CLASS 67 AND 68 LOCOMOTIVES

Andrew Cole

A big thank you to Steve Harrow and to Tony Cole for supplying some photographs for this publication, and for allowing their use. Their images are indicated with (SH) and (TC) respectively.

First published 2019

Amberley Publishing
The Hill, Stroud
Gloucestershire, GL5 4EP

www.amberley-books.com

Copyright © Andrew Cole, 2019

The right of Andrew Cole to be identified as the Author of this work has been asserted in accordance with the Copyrights, Designs and Patents Act 1988.

ISBN 978 1 4456 6174 2 (print)
ISBN 978 1 4456 6175 9 (ebook)

All rights reserved. No part of this book may be reprinted or reproduced or utilised in any form or by any electronic, mechanical or other means, now known or hereafter invented, including photocopying and recording, or in any information storage or retrieval system, without the permission in writing from the Publishers.

British Library Cataloguing in Publication Data.
A catalogue record for this book is available from the British Library.

Origination by Amberley Publishing.
Printed in the UK.

Introduction

Despite being separated in build dates by over a decade, the Class 67 and Class 68 locomotives share some similarities. Thirty Class 67 locomotives were ordered by EWS for delivery from 1999 onwards. They were built by Meinfesa in Valencia, Spain, under contract to General Motors.

The locomotives were ordered to replace the ageing Class 47 locomotives on the lucrative Royal Mail contract, which required reliable locomotives to deliver the mail trains on time. They were fitted with similar engines to the Class 66 locomotives that were also ordered by EWS. The class were fitted with jumper cables to enable them to be used in push-pull mode with a PCV at the other end of the train.

The Class 68 locomotives were also built in Valencia, with Vossloh España being responsible for their construction. Meinfesa became part of the Vossloh group in 2005. The Class 68s resemble the Class 67s in many ways, from their Bo-Bo design and their large one-piece windscreen. So far, thirty-four Class 68 locomotives have been ordered by DRS, with options for follow-up orders.

When EWS lost the Royal Mail contract, they were left with a fleet of locomotives that were seriously underused. Fortunately, the locos managed to find a home on charter trains, and were also leased short-term to passenger TOCs for additional capacity use. The class were used by First Great Western, Chiltern and Wrexham & Shropshire for a while, but their use on all three has since ended. Two members of the class were sold to Colas Rail Freight in 2017 for use on high-speed track-recording trains.

The class were also to be found regularly working the First ScotRail overnight sleeper services in Scotland, but they have since been replaced by the Class 73/9 locomotives. Their only regular work at present is on the East Coast Thunderbird duties, strategically being placed along the length of the route in case of failures. A couple of the class are also in use with Arriva Trains Wales, but with the franchise due to change in 2018, only time will tell if they are to be retained. Two members of the class are also used on Royal Train duties, and have been painted into the corresponding livery.

The Class 68 locomotives were intended as a mixed-traffic locomotive, being equally at home on freight workings as well as passenger workings. The class are currently utilised by several TOCs, including Abellio ScotRail out of Edinburgh Waverley and Chiltern Railways out of London Marylebone. A major contract with TransPennine Express is due to start in 2018, using up to fourteen members of the class on Liverpool Lime Street to Newcastle and Middlesbrough services.

For two classes of locomotives with relatively small numbers, the locos have carried many different liveries over the years, including Royal Train purple and those used by EWS, DB Cargo, Caledonian Sleeper, Arriva Trains Wales, Wrexham & Shropshire, Colas Rail Freight, Belmond British Pullman, Direct Rail Services, Abellio ScotRail, Chiltern Main Line and TransPennine Express. Both classes have many years life ahead of them, although declining traffic levels has resulted in a small number of Class 67 locomotives being stored.

This book aims to show both classes of locomotives in everyday use, from the early days on Royal Mail traffic, through to today. The book is not intended as an in-depth technical description of the classes, more a set of favourite photographs of these very versatile locomotives, which I hope you will enjoy.

No. 67001, 5 June 2000
No. 67001 is seen passing Washwood Heath, on the outskirts of Birmingham, with a Royal Mail working heading for Birmingham New Street, and eventually the South West. Birmingham New Street was always a hive of activity at night, with a procession of mail trains passing through.

No. 67001, 19 February 2001

No. 67001 is seen stabled in front of the admin building at Saltley, Birmingham. The Class 67s were never common visitors to Saltley, although they passed the depot regularly on Royal Mail traffic. Note that by this time No. 67001 has received the name *Night Mail*.

No. 67001, 2 July 2008

No. 67001 is seen on the Aston to Stechford line in Birmingham while propelling a Wrexham & Shropshire working from London Marylebone to Wrexham. This operator was a short-lived open-access operator who ran a few services each day using hired Class 67 and Mark III carriages.

No. 67001, 6 August 2009
No. 67001 is seen stabled at Doncaster while on an East Coast Thunderbird duty. There are a few Class 67 locomotives at strategic locations on the East Coast to help out in need of train failure, and they are ideally suited to the role, with their high top speed and haulage capabilities.

No. 67001, 13 August 2013
No. 67001 is seen arriving at Hereford with an Arriva Trains Wales working from Holyhead through to Cardiff Central via Shrewsbury. There were three Class 67s repainted into Arriva blue livery for passenger turns, and they were used with Mark III carriages, complete with a driving van trailer at the other end.

No. 67001, 10 March 2015

No. 67001 arrives at Manchester Piccadilly with an Arriva Trains Wales passenger turn. The Class 67s are ideally suited to this type of role, and after the loss of the Royal Mail contract their workload decreased, leaving plenty of locos available for short-term hire.

No. 67002, 6 August 2000

No. 67002 is seen on display at the 2000 Old Oak Common open day. This loco had not long been named *Special Delivery*, and within a couple of months it would be involved in a serious collision at Lawrence Hill, Bristol, when it collided with a coal train, mounting the wagons and colliding with an overbridge.

No. 67002, 26 October 2000

No. 67002 *Special Delivery* is seen stabled at Plymouth, waiting to take up service on the evening's postal workings. This shot was taken just six days before its accident in Bristol, which took it out of service for two years.

No. 67002, 13 August 2005

No. 67002 is seen approaching Nuneaton with a rake of Network Rail autoballaster wagons in tow. Fully repaired and back in service, No. 67002 still carries its *Special Delivery* nameplates, despite the Royal Mail traffic ceasing in 2004.

No. 67002, 10 November 2017

No. 67002 is seen stabled at Bescot near to the ballast stockpile. No. 67002 was one of the three Class 67 locomotives chosen to carry Arriva Trains Wales blue livery for use on their passenger workings, although in this view the loco is looking a little worse for wear.

No. 67003, 10 January 2001

No. 67003 stands on the through road at Bristol Temple Meads with a rake of Royal Mail carriages. Bristol was another large postal hub, with a large facility located next to the station, and all platforms had lift access to a bridge that connected the two. Today, the facility has been closed and the lifts and bridge removed.

No. 67003, 9 August 2001
No. 67003 is seen moving onto one of the sidings at the back of Plymouth station. No. 67003 was the first Class 67 to arrive in the UK from Spain, arriving towards the end on 1999, and moved from Newport to Toton on 28 October.

No. 67003, 25 July 2002
No. 67003 is seen having arrived at Plymouth along with Class 47 No. 47759 at the head of a china clay working from St Blazey. These moves were a way of getting locomotives back to Plymouth without the need of a light engine move.

No. 67003, 8 August 2008
No. 67003 is seen approaching Clapham Junction while hauling the VSOE rake of Pullman carriages. These day excursions start from London Victoria and use Class 67 locomotives due to their increased availability. Recently, DB Cargo have repainted two locomotives to match the coaching stock.

No. 67003, 16 September 2015
No. 67003 is seen stabled at Edinburgh Waverley while on an East Coast Thunderbird duty. This was the third Class 67 to be repainted into Arriva Trains Wales blue livery, but when not required on such duties, they can be found on other workings.

No. 67003, 30 December 2016

No. 67003 lurks behind the wall at Crewe while propelling a rake of Arriva Trains Wales Mark III carriages out of the station. Time will tell if the new operator of the Welsh franchise KeolisAmey will retain these locomotives and workings.

No. 67003, 29 August 2017

No. 67003 is seen carrying the attractive Arriva Trains Wales blue livery while stabled at Bescot. This view shows how DB Cargo have started to apply the running numbers on the secondman's cabside, rather than the more usual position of on the driver's cabside.

No. 67004, 23 November 2000

No. 67004 *Post Haste* is seen stabled at Saltley Depot, along with a Class 66 locomotive. Nos 73138 and 86419 have carried similar names to No. 67004 over the years.

No. 67004, 26 July 2002

No. 67004 *Post Haste* is seen again while on one of the through roads at Plymouth station with a rake of Royal Mail carriages. The Class 67s were introduced by EWS to eliminate the older and less reliable Class 47/7 locomotives from this traffic due to its time-sensitive nature. However, they would only be used for four years before the traffic was lost to road transport.

No. 67004, 13 August 2005

No. 67004 is seen arriving at Nuneaton while hauling the Northern Belle rake of carriages. Class 67 locomotives were regular performers on these workings due to their high speed and ETH capabilities, but the haulage contract passed to Direct Rail Services, who now use their Class 57 or 68 locomotives on these workings.

No. 67004, 4 August 2015 (SH)

No. 67004 is seen approaching Spean Bridge while working the 19.50 Caledonian Sleeper from Inverness to London Euston via Edinburgh Waverley. This service will join up with portions from Aberdeen and Fort William at Edinburgh. No. 67004 carries Caledonian Sleeper livery – one of only two Class 67s to do so – and is seen with the name *Cairn Gorm*.

No. 67005, 13 June 2000
No. 67005 rests in one of the bay platforms at Plymouth station. This view was taken before the locomotive was named *Queen's Messenger*.

No. 67005, 22 March 2004
No. 67005 is seen at London King's Cross while on an East Coast Thunderbird duty. The loco is seen now carrying Royal claret livery, as it was dedicated to the Royal Train. This was the first version of the livery it carried, with a yellow stripe at the bottom. It still retains its *Queen's Messenger* nameplates.

No. 67005, 20 October 2014

No. 67005 *Queen's Messenger* is seen stabled at Bescot. By this time, the yellow stripe had given way to a red and orange stripe, and the loco has received EWS logos on the cabside. Bescot is responsible for sprucing the two Royal Class 67 locomotives when they are needed on the Royal Train.

No. 67005, 17 June 2017

No. 67005 *Queen's Messenger* is seen stabled at Bescot, having now received the third version of Royal claret livery, which now includes a bright red stripe. The EWS logos have been replaced with DB Cargo ones

No. 67005, 7 July 2017 (TC)

No. 67005 *Queen's Messenger* is seen at Worcester, having arrived with the VSOE rake of Pullman carriages for stabling. EWS-liveried Class 67 No. 67021 was coupled to the other end of the formation.

No. 67005, 11 December 2017

No. 67005 is seen stabled at Bescot following a heavy fall of snow just before Christmas. The loco still retains its *Queen's Messenger* nameplates, and various cast embellishments on the bodyside.

No. 67006, 2 April 2002

Along with classmate No. 67007, No. 67006 arrives at Plymouth from St Blazey. At the time, the EWS locomotives normally stabled in and around the station, but if exams or minor repairs were due, then they would go to St Blazey.

Nos 67006 and 67005, 7 June 2017

Nos 67006 and 67005 are seen stabled together outside the newly erected shed at Bescot Depot. The shed is a replacement for the old brick building that had been demolished previously. Both locomotives carry Royal claret livery and the names *Royal Sovereign* and *Queen's Messenger* respectively.

No. 67006, 22 November 2017

No. 67006 *Royal Sovereign* is seen stabled in the yard at Bescot. This view shows the *Royal Sovereign* nameplate and also the cast crests on the bodyside. The Class 67 locomotives were built by Meinfesa in Valencia, Spain.

No. 67006, 11 December 2017

No. 67006 stands in the freezing cold at Bescot following an overnight fall of snow. The loco is seen still with its *Royal Sovereign* name, and stands in the company of Class 66 No. 66012. The name is also carried by Class 87 No. 87002.

No. 67007, 19 April 2000

No. 67007 passes Washwood Heath with a Royal Mail working, heading for Birmingham New Street. The loco is still brand new, having not long been unloaded from Newport, and is complete with that new-look shine.

No. 67007, 28 May 2000

No. 67007 is seen stabled at St Blazey Depot, Cornwall, awaiting its next turn of duty. It is seen along with a Class 47/7, the locos that the Class 67s helped eliminate from Royal Mail workings. Also note the Mark I Travelling Post Office vehicle, No. 80414, to the right.

No. 67007, 2 April 2002

No. 67007 is seen having arrived at Plymouth, ready to take up service on the evening's Royal Mail traffic. The loco had been hauled from St Blazey by classmate No. 67006, hence the tail lamp fitted.

No. 67007, 19 July 2013 (TC)

No. 67007 is seen at Fort William, having arrived with a portion of the overnight Caledonian Sleeper from London Euston. The loco will shunt the carriages into the adjacent sidings for them to be stabled and prepared for the evening's run back to London. Note the Scottish flag on the front of the loco. There were only five Class 67s able to work these portions, as they were the only members of the class fitted with RETB cab signalling equipment.

No. 67008, 9 May 2000

No. 67008 is seen at Plymouth along with a Class 47/7. The locos would stable up during the day, then shunt round onto their postal trains, ready to head towards either London or to the North.

No. 67008, 2 June 2000

No. 67008 is seen having arrived at Exeter St David's while on a Royal Mail working. The coaches are being unloaded, and the 67 will soon set off again, stopping at various places along the way, including Bristol, Cheltenham Spa and Birmingham New Street. The large buildings behind No. 67008 have since been demolished.

No. 67008, 8 February 2013

No. 67008 is seen at Bescot, having arrived as part of a freight working behind Class 66 No. 66221. Locomotives are usually transferred between depots as part of a freight working, with regular moves taking place between Crewe, Bescot and Toton.

No. 67008, 25 October 2017

No. 67008 stands at Newcastle station while on an East Coast Thunderbird duty. There are various Class 67 locomotives stabled up and down the East Coast on such duties, including at Edinburgh, Doncaster and London King's Cross, as well as here, at Newcastle.

No. 67009, 1 August 2001

No. 67009 is seen stabled at Plymouth, ready for the night's postal turns. Note how the loco is coupled to one of the former Class 307 driving cars that had been rebuilt as a propelling control vehicle (PCV). These helped eliminate the need for locos to run round as they could work in push-pull mode.

No. 67009, 3 May 2013

No. 67009 is seen being shunted at Bescot by the yard pilot, Class 08 No. 08865. The Class 67 had arrived as part of a freight working, being moved from one depot to another. There is no longer a Class 08 stationed at Bescot, with all shunt moves now being completed by either a Class 60 or Class 66 locomotive.

No. 67009, 22 July 2013

No. 67009 is seen on one of the goods loops at Bescot yard. Of note in the background is the newly delivered Railvac machine. In the background, where the ballast wagons are being unloaded is where the locomotives used to stable in British Rail days.

No. 67010, 9 June 2000

No. 67010 is seen stabled at Plymouth along with another class member. No. 67010 would go on to receive the name *Unicorn*.

No. 67010, 31 May 2002

No. 67010 *Unicorn* is seen arriving at Plymouth while double-heading a china clay working from St Blazey. It is seen working in tandem with classmate No. 67020. The china clay hopper wagons were based on the MGR hoppers, and all have now been withdrawn.

No. 67010, 16 January 2013

No. 67010 passes through Tyseley station while heading for Birmingham Moor Street with a Chiltern Mainline passenger working. There were four Class 67 locomotives originally painted into Wrexham & Shropshire silver livery that were used by Chiltern, with No. 67010 being added later as an additional locomotive.

No. 67010, 30 October 2014

No. 67010 is seen on the buffer stops at Birmingham Moor Street, having arrived with a terminating Chiltern Mainline working from London Marylebone. The DB Class 67 locomotives were to be replaced on these workings by DRS Class 68 locomotives.

No. 67010, 26 January 2018

No. 67010 is seen on the back through road at Doncaster. The loco had been on an East Coast Thunderbird duty and had been used to rescue a failed Virgin Trains East Coast rake of Mark IV carriages, complete with Class 91 No. 91114 *Durham Cathedral* on the back. Note the extra wording on the side of No. 67010.

No. 67011, 9 May 2000
No. 67011 is seen arriving at Plymouth station with a Royal Mail working. This used to be an everyday occurrence, until the loss of the Royal Mail contract in 2004.

No. 67011, 13 August 2004
No. 67011 stands in the sidings opposite Doncaster station while on Thunderbird duty. Note the former Doncaster Works test train behind – a familiar sight at Doncaster for many years.

No. 67012, 29 October 2002

No. 67012 stands on one of the through roads at Plymouth at the head of a Royal Mail postal working. The introduction of the Class 67 locomotives on these workings helped improve the punctuality of these time-sensitive services.

No. 67012, 25 July 2008

No. 67012 is seen passing over the main Birmingham to Derby main line at Washwood Heath while at the head of a Wrexham & Shropshire working to London Marylebone. These workings were short-lived, but four locomotives were repainted into Wrexham & Shropshire livery, and No. 67012 was named *A Shropshire Lad*.

No. 67012, 22 July 2014
No. 67012 *A Shropshire Lad* is seen at Bescot in the consist of a freight working. By this time, the loco had lost its Wrexham & Shropshire branding, but still retained its nameplate.

No. 67013, 5 September 2012
No. 67013 rests on the buffers at Birmingham Moor Street, having arrived with a Chiltern Mainline working from London Marylebone. This loco was one of the four to carry Wrexham & Shropshire livery, but lost the branding when the company ceased trading. It also carries the name *Dyfrbont Pontcysylite*.

No. 67013, 6 February 2013

No. 67013 *Dyfrbont Pontcysyllite* passes through Tyseley station with a Chiltern Mainline working to Birmingham Moor Street. The contract to provide locomotives for the workings would eventually pass to DRS, who now use Class 68 locomotives.

No. 67014, 6 February 2004

No. 67014 is seen at dusk at Saltley Depot, Birmingham. The Class 67s were built by Meinfesa in Spain, and were supplied with Electro-Motive engines, generators and traction motors.

No. 67014, 23 August 2007

No. 67014 is seen passing through Doncaster station on the main Up fast, heading for the nearby Carr Depot. The class were regular visitors to Doncaster, passing through on postal work, and were also based there on East Coast Thunderbird duties.

No. 67014, 19 May 2015 (TC)

No. 67014 is seen arriving at Stourbridge Junction station from the nearby sidings. At this time, many of the Chiltern workings were in the hands of DRS Class 68 locomotives, with just the odd DB Schenker Class 67 being used as cover. No. 67014 was named *Thomas Telford* when in Wrexham & Shropshire use.

No. 67014, 8 December 2016

No. 67014 is seen ready to depart from Bescot, dead attached to Class 66 No. 66009. This was working its way to Toton for repairs from Crewe Electric Depot.

No. 67014, 22 February 2017

No. 67014 is seen propelling a rake of Arriva Trains Wales Mark III carriages out of Manchester Piccadilly. The rake consisted of four tourist standard open (TSO) vehicles and a driving van trailer.

No. 67014, 15 June 2017
No. 67014 is seen on an East Coast Thunderbird duty at Newcastle station. The loco still retains its former Wrexham & Shropshire livery, but has lost its *Thomas Telford* nameplates. The name was previously carried by Class 47 No. 47590.

No. 67015, 26 July 2002
No. 67015 is seen stabled at Plymouth station, awaiting its next turn of duty. It is seen coupled to a propelling control vehicle (PCV), which was rebuilt from a former Class 307 driving car. Also note the EWS-liveried Class 08 stabled on the adjacent siding.

No. 67015, 19 September 2002

No. 67015 rests in the centre road at Plymouth station, waiting to take up its evening Royal Mail departure. Of note is the tail lamp in the windscreen of the locomotive, as well as the red tail lamps displayed on the back of the High Security Brake Van (NBA) next to the loco.

No. 67015, 2 July 2008

No. 67015 propels a Wrexham & Shropshire working on the Aston to Stechford line in Birmingham, while heading for Wrexham. The loco carries Wrexham & Shropshire livery, and also the name *David J. Lloyd*. The Mark III carriages belonged to Cargo-D, and carry British Rail blue and grey livery.

No. 67015, 5 July 2008

No. 67015 *David J. Lloyd* makes a station call at Wolverhampton while working a Wrexham & Shropshire working from London Marylebone to Wrexham. These services were not allowed to call at Birmingham New Street; instead, they had to go via the Aston to Stechford line.

No. 67015, 18 May 2009 (TC)

No. 67015 *David J. Lloyd* is seen propelling a couple of British Rail-liveried Mark III carriages through Northampton. The consist was heading to Wembley to take up service with Wrexham & Shropshire.

No. 67015, 3 September 2014

No. 67015 is seen stabled at Bescot Depot, Walsall. The loco is seen still carrying its Wrexham & Shropshire livery, and also its name, *David J. Lloyd*, but it would soon lose both, with the livery changing to DB Schenker red.

No. 67015, 22 March 2016 (TC)

No. 67015 stands at Edinburgh Waverley while at the head of a Caledonian Sleeper working. The loco now carries DB Schenker livery, and is seen alongside classmate No. 67011, which still carries as-delivered EWS maroon livery. Today, DB Cargo no longer run these services, with Caledonian Sleeper services now using GBRf Class 73/9 and Class 92 locomotives.

No. 67016, 19 September 2002

No. 67016 is seen stabled at Plymouth, awaiting its northbound Royal Mail working. The Class 67 locomotives took over these workings from the increasingly unreliable Class 47/7s, but would only see four years' service before the parcels traffic was lost to road transport.

No. 67016, 20 March 2003

No. 67016 is seen arriving at Doncaster while on railtour duty, and is hauling a rake of green and cream Mark I carriages. Class 67s were ideal for this type of traffic, with their maximum speed of 125 mph, and also their electric train heating capabilities.

No. 67016, 7 September 2004
No. 67016 is seen stabled at London King's Cross while on an East Coast Thunderbird duty. Today, these sidings have been removed and one line has been extended into the station to create a new platform, Platform 0.

No. 67016, 9 May 2006
No. 67016 is seen still on East Coast Thunderbird duties, but by this time the loco had moved north to Doncaster. The class were originally owned by Angel Trains, but have since been bought outright by DB Cargo.

No. 67016, 2 April 2009
No. 67016 is seen arriving at Bristol Temple Meads. At this time, First Great Western operated a short passenger set that, due to a shortage of serviceable DMUs, was top-and-tailed by Class 67 locomotives along with a set of Riviera Trains Mark II carriages. Classmate No. 67017 *Arrow* is on the other end of the working.

No. 67016, 14 November 2014
No. 67016 is seen stabled at Bescot while carrying as-delivered EWS maroon livery. Note the Scottish flag sticker on the front of the loco – an embellishment added when it was used on sleeper traffic north of the border.

No. 67017, 23 October 2000
No. 67017 stands in one of the south bays at Plymouth, awaiting its next turn of duty. The Class 67 locomotives were built to a Bo-Bo wheel design, rather than the Co-Co design used under the larger Class 66 locomotives.

No. 67017, 8 August 2005
No. 67017 is seen passing through the centre roads at Doncaster with a rake of continental ferry wagons. By this time No. 67017 had received the name *Arrow*, which can be seen on the driver's cabside. To date, just over half of the class either carry names, or have carried them and had them removed.

No. 67017, 2 July 2008

No. 67017 *Arrow* is seen propelling a Wrexham & Shropshire working towards London Marylebone on the Aston to Stechford line in Birmingham. Despite some members of the class receiving Wrexham & Shropshire livery, ordinarily liveried locomotives were also used.

No. 67017, 2 April 2009

No. 67017 *Arrow* is seen again, this time at Bristol Temple Meads. The Class 67 was being used at the time by First Great Western as they were short of serviceable DMUs, with Riviera Trains supplying the Mark II carriages.

No. 67017, 23 May 2013

No. 67017 is seen arriving at its destination station, Birmingham Moor Street, with a Chiltern Mainline working from London Marylebone. At this time, No. 67017 still retained its *Arrow* nameplates.

No. 67018, 13 August 2004

No. 67018 is seen passing through Doncaster on a soaking wet summer's day with a rake of continental ferry wagons. At this time, No. 67018 carried the name *Rapid*, but it would lose this name later on in its career.

No. 67018, 26 May 2007

No. 67018 *Rapid* is seen arriving at Newton Abbott while on a charter working. This comprised a rake of EWS maroon-liveried Mark II carriages, along with a green and cream Mark I buffet car.

No. 67018, 25 October 2013

Now named *Keith Heller*, No. 67018 is seen passing through Tyseley at the head of a Chiltern Mainline working from London Marylebone to Birmingham Moor Street. No. 67018 is seen carrying a unique DB Schenker livery; indeed, this livery was so unique that it was only carried by No. 67018.

No. 67018, 3 February 2015
No. 67018 is seen stabled at Wembley yard still carrying its unique DB Schenker livery. This view also shows the name *Keith Heller* off nicely.

No. 67018, 4 May 2017
No. 67018 *Keith Heller* is seen stabled at Bescot, complete with its maple leaf DB Schenker livery. Canadian Keith Heller was the former chairman of EWS and DB Schenker, with the maple leaf being a means of honouring him.

No. 67018, 16 June 2018

No. 67018 *Keith Heller* is seen stabled at Bescot. The loco is coupled to a Mark I barrier vehicle, which at the time was in use with brand-new Bombardier-built EMU sets – in particular, the Elizabeth line Class 345 units.

No. 67019, 9 May 2000

No. 67019 is seen departing from the sidings at Plymouth, being dragged by a former Rail Express Systems Class 47/7 locomotive. No. 67019 still retains its brand-new shine, as it had not long been in traffic.

No. 67019, 31 May 2004

No. 67019 is seen on display at the National Railway Museum during a special event in 2004 called York Railfest, which was held to celebrate several anniversaries that occurred that year.

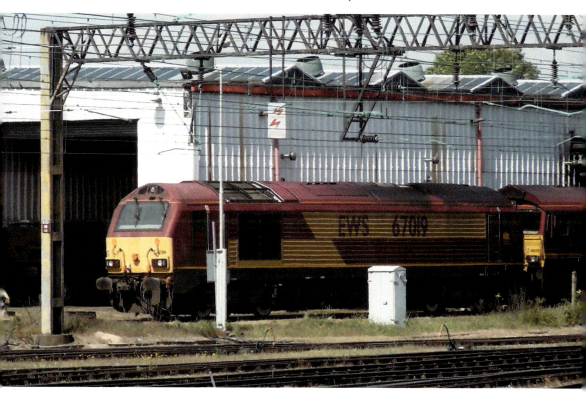

No. 67019, 3 June 2013

No. 67019 is seen at Bescot, awaiting its turn on the fuel pumps. Since this shot was taken, the old diesel depot behind has been completely demolished, and it had been replaced with a new metal construction.

No. 67020, 31 May 2002

Along with classmate No. 67010 *Unicorn*, No. 67020 is seen at Plymouth, having arrived at the head of a china clay working. These workings were a way of getting extra locos to Plymouth from St Blazey, where they had been for maintenance.

No. 67020, 24 March 2009

No. 67020 is seen stabled at London King's Cross while on an East Coast Thunderbird duty. This side-on view shows the loco off a treat, including the see-through grills at the right-hand side of the loco and the split yellow stripe carried by the Class 67s.

No. 67020, 21 January 2015

No. 67020 passes through Tyseley as it heads for Birmingham Moor Street. By the time this shot was taken, the writing was on the wall for DB Schenker-hauled Chiltern Mainline workings, with Direct Rail Services having won the contract, and the Class 67s would be replaced by Class 68s.

No. 67020, 4 February 2015

No. 67020 is seen propelling its rake of Chiltern Mainline Mark III carriages out of Birmingham Moor Street, heading for the sidings just outside the station. No. 67020 is seen still carrying the EWS maroon livery it was delivered in from Spain in 2000.

No. 67020, 11 February 2015

No. 67020 is seen stabled in the sidings just to the south of Birmingham Moor Street. The locos could stay on these workings for weeks at a time, as indicated by these two shots being taken a week apart.

No. 67021, 29 June 2015

No. 67021 stands at London King's Cross while on East Coast Thunderbird duty. With the opening of Platform 0 at King's Cross, a new siding was laid for the Thunderbird loco, on which No. 67021 sits.

No. 67021, 8 July 2017 (TC)
No. 67021 is seen stabled on Worcester stabling point, coupled to the VSOE rake of elderly Pullman carriages. The formation is seen in top-and-tail formation, with classmate No. 67005 *Queen's Messenger* attached to the other end.

No. 67021, 5 March 2018 (SH)
No. 67021 is seen stabled at Bescot. By this time, the loco had been repainted into Pullman livery. Having received Belmond British Pullman logos, this loco was repainted, along with classmate No. 67024, for use on the Belmond Pullman services.

No. 67022, 25 August 2000

No. 67022 is seen backing onto a rake of Royal Mail postal carriages at Plymouth. The first carriage is a former Class 307 driving car, which was rebuilt as a propelling control vehicle (PCV).

No. 67022, 29 October 2002

No. 67022 rests on the back sidings at Plymouth, ready for an evening departure on a Royal Mail working. There would be just over a year's service for these workings remaining, before the contract was lost in 2004.

No. 67022, 12 March 2015

No. 67022 is seen stabled on London King's Cross while on East Coast Thunderbird duties. The Class 67 locomotives were built by Meinfesa in Valencia, Spain, and were delivered at the same time as the Canadian-built Class 66 locomotives.

No. 67022, 8 November 2015

While still carrying EWS maroon livery, No. 67022 is seen stabled at Bescot with classmates Nos 67014 and 67028. While Class 67s certainly visited Bescot, it was not in great numbers, so to get three together was quite rare.

No. 67022, 14 December 2016

No. 67022 arrives at Hereford while hauling an Arriva Trains Wales passenger working from Holyhead to Cardiff Central. The low morning sunshine shows off the front of the locomotive well, including the swing head buckeye coupling.

No. 67022, 16 June 2017

No. 67022 arrives at Manchester Piccadilly while hauling a rake of Arriva Trains Wales Mark III carriages. Over time, this class of locomotives never realised their potential, especially after the Royal Mail traffic was lost.

No. 67023, 30 July 2002

No. 67023 is seen stabled at Plymouth, having arrived with an overnight Royal Mail working. This locomotive would be one of two sold by DB Cargo. It is currently operated by Colas Rail Freight, and is used on Network Rail high-speed test trains, now having been named *Stella*.

No. 67023, 19 September 2016

No. 67023 is seen stabled at London King's Cross while on East Coast Thunderbird duties. Four months after this shot, the locomotive was sold to Colas Rail Freight.

No. 67024, 11 July 2000

Not long after entering service, No. 67024 is seen stabled on Plymouth station, and it is still spotlessly clean. Later on in its DB Cargo career, this locomotive received Belmond British Pullman livery, similar to classmate No. 67021.

No. 67024, 25 March 2016

No. 67024 is seen on East Coast Thunderbird duties at London King's Cross. These locomotives are only pressed into service to help stricken trains, in order to clear the main line.

No. 67025, 13 June 2000
No. 67025 is seen stabled at Plymouth at the head of an overnight Royal Mail working. This locomotive had only been in the country for three weeks when this shot was taken, and is still looking very respectable.

No. 67025, 23 August 2001
No. 67025 is seen at Plymouth, waiting to depart from one of the back sidings. This locomotive would go on to become one of the seventeen members of the class that were named, with No. 67025 carrying the name *Western Star*.

No. 67025, 22 August 2002
No. 67025 is seen having arrived at Plymouth while double-heading a china clay working with classmate No. 67029. By this time, No. 67025 had been named *Western Star*. This name was previously carried by Britannia steam locomotive No. 70025.

No. 67025, 13 August 2004
No. 67025 *Western Star* is seen passing through Doncaster on the Up fast line while hauling a Network Rail MPV. This view shows the position of the nameplate on the cabside off nicely.

No. 67026, 11 July 2000
No. 67026 rests in the through sidings at Plymouth as it waits to depart with an evening's Royal Mail postal service.

No. 67026, 20 December 2001
No. 67026 passes Washwood Heath, on the outskirts of Birmingham, with a Royal Mail postal working for the South West. This would almost certainly have been an extra service, with the Christmas postal rush being in full swing at the time.

No. 67026, 27 August 2002

No. 67026 is seen racing through Totnes station at the start of its long journey northwards with another postal working. The train has just descended Rattery Bank, with the last of the coaches just having come off the bank.

No. 67026, 23 March 2012

No. 67026 is seen at Walsall station while being hauled towards Bescot by classmate No. 67006 *Royal Sovereign*. By this time, No. 67026 had just been repainted into its unique Diamond Jubilee livery, which was matched in its new name – *Diamond Jubilee*.

No. 67026, 11 May 2012

No. 67026 is seen just south of Bescot Yard. This locomotive was chosen to carry a special livery to commemorate the Queen's Diamond Jubilee, and it acted as a back-up locomotive to the two Royal Claret-liveried Class 67s.

No. 67026, 13 June 2013

No. 67026 *Diamond Jubilee* is seen at London King's Cross while on an East Coast Thunderbird duty. When not required on the Royal Train, the three special Class 67 locomotives could find work on any number of mundane duties.

No. 67026, 16 September 2015

No. 67026 *Diamond Jubilee* is seen at Edinburgh Waverley on a special working to Tweedbank. The loco is seen on the rear of the Scottish Railway Preservation Society's rake of maroon-liveried Mark I carriages, with A4 Pacific No. 60009 *Union of South Africa* leading.

No. 67027, 1 August 2013

No. 67027 *Rising Star* is seen stabled at London King's Cross. The name carried by this Class 67 was previously carried by Britannia steam locomotive No. 70027, and it is a nice touch that No. 67027 follows on from No. 70027.

No. 67027, 25 August 2014
No. 67027 is seen stabled at Stourbridge Junction while coupled to a rake of Chiltern Mainline-liveried Mark III carriages. By now No. 67027 had been fully repainted into DB Schenker red livery, and had lost its *Rising Star* nameplates.

No. 67027, 25 August 2014
No. 67027 is again seen stabled at Stourbridge Junction. This time it is in company with classmate No. 67018 *Keith Heller*, and both locomotives carry DB Schenker livery, although No. 67018 displays an earlier version with a red skirt, whereas No. 67027 carries a grey skirt.

No. 67027, 11 September 2016

No. 67027 is seen stabled by the fuel roads at Toton Depot. No. 67027 was in storage at this time, and would soon be sold to Colas Rail Freight for use on Network Rail high-speed test trains. In doing so, it would lose its DB Schenker red livery in favour of Colas orange and yellow.

No. 67027, 10 February 2017 (SH)

No. 67027 passes Wichnor Junction on the back of a Network Rail working from Crewe to Derby. The train consisted of three former Virgin Trains Mark III driving van trailers, and classmate No. 67023 is hauling the consist. Both locomotives carry Colas Rail Freight livery.

No. 67027, 23 March 2017 (SH)

No. 67027 passes Coleshill Parkway on the back of a Network Rail test train heading for Leicester. To date, this Class 67 and classmate No. 67023 are the only two that have been sold by DB Cargo to other operators.

No. 67027, 1 June 2017

No. 67027 is seen at Platform 5 at Northampton with another Network Rail test train. Unusually, the consist was led by Class 73 No. 73951. Since this shot was taken, No. 67027 has been named *Charlotte*.

No. 67028, 23 August 2007
No. 67028 stands in the West Yard at Doncaster while on Thunderbird duty. Of note is the One Anglia-liveried Class 47, No. 47813, behind.

No. 67028, 28 February 2016 (SH)
No. 67028 is seen having just departed from Coventry Arena station while hauling a rugby extra from Nuneaton to Coventry via the Ricoh Arena. The train consisted of six former Anglia-liveried Mark II carriages and fellow Class 67 No. 67006 *Royal Sovereign* is on the rear.

No. 67028, 6 April 2016

No. 67028 is seen stabled in the Down engineer's yard at Bescot. Alongside is Class 66 No. 66058, which has been repainted into DB Cargo livery. This would prove to be short-lived, however, as it was later sold to GB Railfreight, who renumbered it No. 66783 and had it repainted into a special Biffa livery.

No. 67028, 4 May 2018

No. 67028 is seen stabled at Bescot. By now, the loco had been repainted into full DB Cargo red livery, and had also received some next-generation rail freight decals on the bodyside.

No. 67029, 30 July 2002
No. 67029 is seen stabled in the centre road at Plymouth with a Royal Mail postal working. This loco only carried EWS maroon and gold livery for around four years, before it was chosen to haul the EWS company trains, being repainted silver in the process.

No. 67029, 22 August 2002
No. 67029 is seen having arrived at Plymouth in the consist of a china clay working, being hauled by classmate No. 67025 *Western Star*.

No. 67029, 30 April 2005

No. 67029 is seen stabled at Bescot, having just been released from Toton following a repaint into its special silver livery. This locomotive was used to power the EWS company trains, but these workings were few and far between, so it could always be found on other traffic.

No. 67029, 30 April 2015

No. 67029 is seen at Proofhouse Junction, just outside Birmingham New Street, while hauling a Network Rail test train. The train also has classmate No. 67012 *A Shropshire Lad* on the rear. By this time, No. 67029 had received the name *Royal Diamond*.

No. 67029, 7 May 2016
No. 67029 stands on the buffer stops at London Euston on the rear of a charter working. The loco received the name *Royal Diamond* in 2007 at Rugeley Trent Valley, as the plaque underneath the name commemorates.

No. 67029, 16 July 2016
No. 67029 is again stabled at Bescot, still carrying its unique silver livery. Of note is that, over time, the EWS beastie logos were removed and were replaced with a large DB logo, which didn't have the same effect as the EWS logo.

No. 67030, 1 September 2000

No. 67030 is seen stabled at Plymouth. This was the last member of the class to be delivered, and when this shot was taken it had only been in the country for one month, following delivery from Spain.

No. 67030, 19 September 2015

No. 67030 is seen stabled at Edinburgh Waverley along with two Caledonian Sleeper Mark II carriages. DB Cargo would subsequently lose the contract for hauling the Caledonian Sleeper to GBRf, who now use Class 73/9 locomotives on these workings.

No. 67030, 14 August 2017

No. 67030 rests at London King's Cross while on an East Coast Thunderbird duty. Since the loss of the Royal Mail contract, the Class 67 locomotives have never realised their potential, with charter work and test trains being their staple work, but with their top speed of 125 mph, they were always capable of much more.

No. 68001, 29 April 2015

No. 68001 *Evolution* is seen passing through Rugeley Trent Valley while heading southwards as a light engine move. No. 68001 was displayed at the InnoTrans exhibition in Berlin, Germany, in 2014 before being shipped to the UK.

No. 68001, 11 June 2015

No. 68001 is seen stabled at Stourbridge Junction. The loco was based here for driver training duty, as the class were to be used by Chiltern Railways on their main line workings to London Marylebone. No. 68001 carries the name *Evolution*.

No. 68001, 27 May 2016

No. 68001 *Evolution* slowly passes through Leicester station with a rake of empty Network Rail ballast wagons. This working had originated at Basford Hall, Crewe, and was nearly at journey's end at Mountsorrel.

No. 68001, 22 July 2017

No. 68001 *Evolution* is seen on display at the 2017 Carlisle Kingmoor open day. The Class 68 locomotives are all operated by Direct Rail Services, who have two depots – Carlisle Kingmoor and Gresty Road, Crewe.

No. 68002, 31 March 2016

No. 68002 *Intrepid* is seen departing Wolverhampton station as part of a Network Rail test train. The coach immediately behind is No. 975091 *Mentor*, which is used to check the overhead wires. Classmate No. 68004 *Rapid* is leading the consist.

No. 68003, 16 September 2015

No. 68003 *Astute* is seen at Haymarket while on a passenger working. There is a requirement from ScotRail to use two Class 68 and Mark II carriages on peak-time commuter workings out of Edinburgh Waverley – one to Glenrothes with Thornton station, and the other to Cardenden.

No. 68004, 20 October 2014

No. 68004 *Rapid* is seen on the approach to Walsall station while hauling a Network Rail continuous welded rail train. These trains are used to carry long lengths of rail to worksites for the replacement of worn-out track.

No. 68004, 9 September 2016 (SH)

No. 68004 *Rapid* passes over Reedham Swing Bridge with an Anglia working to Norwich. Classmate No. 68024 *Centaur* was attached to the rear. The use of Class 68 locomotives on passenger services around Norwich was the result of a unit shortage following a level crossing accident featuring No. 170204.

No. 68004, 5 September 2017

No. 68004 *Rapid* arrives at Haymarket with a ScotRail working to Edinburgh Waverley. Two Class 68 locomotives carry ScotRail livery, but Direct Rail Services-liveried locomotives are no strangers to these workings either.

No. 68005, 11 February 2015

No. 68005 passes light engine through Water Orton. Situated to the east of Birmingham, this is a very busy station for both freight and passenger workings, and it is where the lines to Derby diverge from the lines to Leicester. No. 68005 carries the name *Defiant*.

No. 68005, 9 November 2015

No. 68005 *Defiant* passes through a gloomy Walsall station on a miserable autumn afternoon with a rake of Network Rail autoballaster wagons in tow. This scene will change forever with the installation of overhead wires as part of the Chase line electrification to Rugeley Trent Valley.

No. 68006, 16 September 2015

No. 68006 *Daring* is seen making a station call at Haymarket while on a ScotRail passenger working. This is one of the two Class 68 locomotives that carry ScotRail livery for these workings, but they don't always appear on them.

No. 68006, 29 April 2016

No. 68006 *Daring* is seen on the approach to Rugeley Trent Valley, having traversed the Chase Line from Bescot. The loco carries ScotRail livery, and is an unusual visitor down south due to it being used on ScotRail passenger workings.

No. 68006, 22 July 2017

No. 68006 *Daring* is seen on display at the 2017 Carlisle Kingmoor open day. This view shows the ScotRail livery off nicely, as well as the unusual position of the running number. Note also the large Vossloh builder's plate in front of the leading bogie.

No. 68007, 15 January 2015

No. 68007 *Valiant* is seen stabled at Bescot, having arrived with a ballast working. This loco only carried Direct Rail Services livery for a short while, with it later receiving ScotRail livery for passenger services north of the border.

No. 68007, 27 January 2015

No. 68007 *Valiant* prepares to depart from Bescot with a rake of Network Rail autoballaster wagons in tow. The Class 68 locomotives are used on all types of DRS traffic, including intermodal and nuclear traffic, and not just on departmental workings.

No. 68007, 24 July 2015 (SH)

No. 68007 *Valiant* is seen arriving at South Gyle with a ScotRail commuter passenger working from Edinburgh Waverley. The locomotive and Mark II carriages carry matching ScotRail livery.

No. 68008, 22 May 2016

No. 68008 *Avenger* is seen stabled at Stourbridge Junction. This is where Chiltern stable their loco-hauled sets at the north end of the route, and they also have a depot at Wembley at the south end. The Class 68 locomotives are operated by DRS, but are owned by Beacon Rail.

No. 68008, 20 July 2016

No. 68008 *Avenger* is seen having arrived at Birmingham Moor Street with a terminating Chiltern Mainline working from London Marylebone. This is one of two extra Class 68 locomotives that are equipped to work these trains, No. 68009 *Titan* being the other, but both still retain full DRS livery.

No. 68010, 23 April 2015 (TC)

No. 68010 is seen departing from Stourbridge Junction while propelling a Chiltern Mainline working through to London Marylebone. The Class 68s are able to be worked remotely by the former Mark III driving van trailer at the other end of the formation.

No. 68010, 29 June 2015

No. 68010 arrives at London Marylebone with a terminating Chiltern Mainline working. There are six dedicated Class 68s used on the Chiltern passenger workings that carry Chiltern livery, and there are two extra locomotives that act as back-up.

No. 68011, 19 May 2015

No. 68011 departs from Birmingham Moor Street with a Chiltern Mainline working to London Marylebone. The Chiltern livery suits these locomotives well. Just above the loco an old steam water column can be seen, with Moor Street having been beautifully restored, resulting in it having a GWR feel to it.

No. 68011, 29 June 2015

No. 68011 stands at London Marylebone, waiting to depart back towards Birmingham Moor Street with a Chiltern Mainline working. The six dedicated locomotives were delivered carrying Chiltern livery, and to date only one of them has received a name.

No. 68012, 20 October 2015
No. 68012 is seen waiting to depart from Bescot engineers' sidings with a rake of Network Rail ballast wagons. The Chiltern-liveried locomotives were used on general freight duties when they were delivered, but were soon dedicated to passenger workings.

No. 68012, 22 July 2017
No. 68012 is seen on display at the 2017 Carlisle Kingmoor open day. The Class 68 locomotives used by Chiltern are devoid of any markings and just carry Chiltern Mainline livery. The open days at Carlisle are held every two years, alternating with the DRS depot at Crewe Gresty Road.

No. 68013, 3 February 2015

No. 68013 is seen coupled to a nuclear flask wagon at Wembley when still relatively new. DRS have their own dedicated compound at Wembley, to allow their locomotives to be securely stabled, and No. 68013 is seen alongside Class 66 No. 66302.

No. 68013, 18 March 2015

No. 68013 is seen at Bescot, having hauled in a Network Rail continuous welded rail train. Despite being dedicated to Chiltern passenger workings, these six locomotives also turn up on freight workings, albeit rarely.

No. 68014, 19 May 2015

No. 68014 is seen at Birmingham Snow Hill, ready to depart for London Marylebone. The Chiltern livery certainly suits these locomotives, and it matches the Mark III carriages well. This photograph was taken during the transition period from DB Cargo Class 67 operation to DRS Class 68 operation.

No. 68014, 10 February 2017

No. 68014 is seen waiting for the road at Northampton while hauling classmate No. 68013 northwards. The Chiltern locomotives are based at Wembley for day-to-day maintenance, but still have to head north to Crewe Gresty Road when heavier exams are required, which is where this duo are heading.

No. 68015, 31 May 2015

No. 68015 is seen acting as a spare locomotive at Stourbridge Junction. In the background, three classmates can be seen: Nos 68011, 68008 and 68014. No. 68008 *Avenger* is one of the two back-up locomotives, and it still carries full DRS livery.

No. 68015, 29 June 2015

No. 68015 is seen arriving at London Marylebone while propelling a Chiltern Railways working into the station. The set of Mark III carriages carry BR blue and grey livery, and were on short-term hire to Chiltern while their own carriages were being refurbished at Doncaster.

No. 68016, 2 June 2016

No. 68016 *Fearless* is seen coupled to a rake of Network Rail autoballaster wagons at Bescot. No. 68016 was the first member of the second batch of Class 68s to arrive in the UK. Despite being built by Stadler, who had brought Vossloh España, they still carry Vossloh builder's plates.

No. 68017, 8 June 2016

No. 68017 *Hornet* is seen stabled at Norwich. At this time, DRS had a contract to supply Anglia Railways with a top-and-tailed short set formed of two Class 68 locomotives and three Mark II carriages, and No. 68017 is seen acting as a spare locomotive for the set.

No. 68018, 14 March 2016

No. 68018 *Vigilant* works northwards through Leicester with a rake of Network Rail ballast wagons, heading for the nearby Mountsorrel works. This train originated at Crewe and, having been filled with ballast, would return later in the day.

No. 68018, 9 August 2017

No. 68018 is seen powering through Longbridge station while double-heading a couple of nuclear flask wagons with classmate No. 68030. This working started in Bridgwater, Somerset, and was heading back towards Crewe. No. 68018 carries the name *Vigilant*, whereas No. 68030 has yet to receive a name.

No. 68018 and No. 68016, 24 May 2018

No. 68018 *Vigilant* and No. 68016 *Fearless* are seen heading past Longbridge turnback sidings while hauling two empty flat wagons from Bridgewater to Crewe. There are always two locomotives used on the nuclear traffic, in case of failure, and the Class 68s have taken over these duties from Class 37 and Class 57 locomotives.

No. 68019, 1 March 2018 (SH)

With classmate No. 68021 *Tireless*, No. 68019 *Brutus* is seen passing Water Orton while being hauled by Class 47 No. 47813. This was part of a move to get the locos to Dollands Moor for testing new TransPennine Mark V stock, but due to paperwork issues the locomotives ended up back at Crewe. TransPennine are due to start using these locomotives and stock on their network in 2018.

No. 68021, 15 September 2016

No. 68021 *Tireless* is seen entering the South Stour tunnel at Birmingham New Street while on the back of a Network Rail test train. These locomotives are ideal for this kind of work, with their high-speed capabilities.

No. 68022, 18 January 2017

No. 68022 *Resolution* is seen on a miserable January day at Bescot. Of note is what appears to be only one working tail light; in fact both are working, as the Class 68 head and tail lights flicker on and off at a high rate, which cannot be seen with the naked eye.

No. 68022, 22 July 2017

No. 68022 *Resolution* is seen in the head shunt just outside Carlisle Kingmoor Depot. This was taken during the open day in 2017, where there were quite a few members of the class on display.

No. 68023, 14 June 2016

No. 68023 *Achilles* is seen at a very wet Bescot, having arrived with a rake of Network Rail sleeper wagons. DRS locomotives do occasionally visit Bescot, but they are not as regular a sight as GBRf or Colas Rail Freight.

No. 68023, 15 June 2016

No. 68023 arrives at Bescot with a rake of ballast wagons. The Class 68 locomotives are equally at home on mundane ballast work as express charter work; indeed, they are a truly mixed-traffic locomotive. No. 68023 carries the name *Achilles*.

No. 68024, 9 September 2016 (SH)

No. 68024 *Centaur* is seen arriving back at Norwich on the back of an Anglia working from Lowestoft. No. 68004 *Rapid* is leading the working, which comprised former Anglia-liveried Mark II carriages.

No. 68026, 22 July 2017

No. 68026 is seen on display at the 2017 Carlisle Kingmoor open day. This was the first locomotive of the third batch of Class 68s delivered to DRS, and it is seen carrying a plain blue livery; as these locomotives were due to be used on the TransPennine working, they will receive TransPennine livery.

No. 68029, 22 July 2017

No. 68029, complete with headboards, is seen inside the shed at Carlisle Kingmoor. Note that, from No. 68026 onwards, the builder's plates are now Stadler rather than Vossloh.

No. 68031, 23 July 2017

No. 68031 is seen on display at The Railway Age, Crewe. This photograph was taken during a small diesel gathering at the heritage centre, with DRS sending No. 68031 to be put on display. The plain blue livery suits this class well.

No. 68032, 4 September 2017

No. 68032 stands at Edinburgh Waverley, having arrived with a ScotRail working. These commuter services work to Glenrothes with Thornton and Cardenden. When this shot was taken No. 68032 had not been in the country long. Its first workings were north of the border.

No. 68032, 5 September 2017

No. 68032 arrives at Haymarket with an early-morning ScotRail commuter working to Edinburgh Waverley. With there being a couple of services in the morning and a couple in the evening, the locomotives can appear on these working for days at a time due to them being stabled at Millerhill when not in use.

No. 68032, 6 January 2018

Alongside classmate No. 68031, No. 68032 is seen stabled at Crewe Gresty Bridge Depot, awaiting its next turn of duty. This short-lived plain blue livery will disappear when the locomotives are painted into TransPennine livery. No. 68032 was the last loco to carry this livery, as Nos 68033 and 68034 were delivered carrying full DRS livery.